the wind blows
through the doors of my heart

the wind blows through the doors of my heart

POEMS

Deborah Digges

ALFRED A. KNOPF   NEW YORK | 2010

Library of Congress Cataloging-in-Publication Data
Digges, Deborah.
The wind blows through the doors of my heart : poems / by Deborah Digges.
p. cm.
"This is a Borzoi book."
ISBN 978-0-307-26846-4
I. Title.
PS3554.I3922W56 2010
811'.54—dc22   2009040675

Manufactured in the United States of America
First Edition

There was youth in us then, a wild hope. It was during those long days that we were all merged into a unity, so that on another planet we shall recognize one another, and the things cry to each other, the cookoo clock and my books to the lean-fleshed cows on the lawn and the sorrowful old Kikuyus: "You also were there. . . ." That bad time blessed us and went away.

—KAREN BLIXEN

contents

editor's note

When Deborah Digges died on April 10, 2009, this volume was well under way and she was revising it with an eye toward its publication in book form. Most of the poems were entirely finished and clean copies had been prepared by her. But in other cases there were multiple versions of a poem still being worked on, or handwritten marginal notes she had made about possible revisions; some new poems were not yet added to her working table of contents. In the text that follows we have endeavored to represent, as nearly as could be determined with the help of her literary estate, her final intentions for each line and each word, and have made up the contents in an order we imagine would have met with her approval. Such a process is by its nature imperfect, and we hope that the poems will find their own life beyond these pages, as Deborah Digges surely intended.

the wind blows
through the doors of my heart

the wind blows
through the doors of my heart

The wind blows
through the doors of my heart.
It scatters my sheet music
that climbs like waves from the piano, free of the keys.
Now the notes stripped, black butterflies,
flattened against the screens.
The wind through my heart
blows all my candles out.
In my heart and its rooms is dark and windy.
From the mantle smashes birds' nests, teacups
full of stars as the wind winds round,
a mist of sorts that rises and bends and blows
or is blown through my rooms of my heart
that shatters the windows,
rakes the bedsheets as though someone
had just made love. And my dresses
they are lifted like brides come to rest
on the bedstead, crucifixes,
dresses tangled in trees in the rooms
of my heart. To save them
I've thrown flowers to fields,
so that someone would pick them up
and know where they came from.

Come the bees now clinging to flowered curtains.
Off with the clothesline pinning anything, my mother's
    trousseau.
It is not for me to say what is this wind
or how it came to blow through the rooms of my heart.
Wing after wing, through the rooms of the dead
the wind does not blow. Nor the basement, no wheezing,
no wind choking the cobwebs in our hair.
It is cool here, quiet, a quilt spread on soil.
But we will never lie down again.

don't cut your hair

Don't cut your hair while your beloved is at sea.
But we could wade into the garden, tie nightgowns up
      between our thighs
and weed between the lilies.
We've rowed, ourselves, seven seasons of ice
toward the advent of the bloom of the wisteria,
slipped silently beyond the buoy bells of alien harbors,
cargoes of hyacinth, still in their shipping beds, blossoming in
      the hold.
O mutinous flowers born adrift
by the swells, clinging to the oarlocks, to be dashed and lifted.
And then to hear the sirens singing, lighting their sisters' way
      into such green,
where, set to work among the crofts and hedgerows,
women weeding, crones stooped among the bell flowers,
brides tying back their veils, bending to weed,
leaning from widows' walks to pots along the eaves
where even up so high weeds can take root.
Women weeding, weeding, kneeling by caves, in prison,
outside the chained and padlocked gates of Eden.
There are still fields where you may come across a
      shipwrecked garden,
a run of cornflowers along a path of stones,

the arbor overcome with roses.
About a chimney a grove several sages, bearded iris
drowning in weeds like lover's hair pulled under by desire
a bracken moon once dragged ashore.
Weed for the ghosts who gardened here.

the birthing

Call out the names in the procession of the loved.
Call from the blood the ancestors here to bear witness
to the day he stopped the car,
we on our way to a great banquet in his honor.
In a field a cow groaned lowing, trying to give birth,
what he called *front leg presentation,*
the calf came out nose first, one front leg dangling from his
    mother.
A fatal sign he said while rolling up the sleeves
of his dress shirt, and climbed the fence.
I watched him thrust his arms entire
into the yet-to-be, where I imagined holy sparrows scattering
in the hall of souls for his big mortal hands just to make way.
With his whole weight he pushed the calf back in the mother
and grasped the other leg tucked up like a closed wing
against the new one's shoulder.
And found a way in the warm dark to bring both legs out
into the world together.
Then heaved and pulled, the cow arching her back.
Until a bull calf, in a whoosh of blood and water,
came falling whole and still onto the meadow.
We rubbed his blackness, bloodying our hands.
The mother licked her newborn, of us oblivious,
until it moved a little, struggled.

I ran to get our coats, mine a green velvet cloak,
and his tuxedo jacket, and worked to rub the new one dry
while he set out to find the farmer.
When it was over, the new calf suckling his mother,
the farmer soon to lead them to the barn,
leaving our coats just where they lay
we huddled in the car.
And then made love toward eternity,
without a word drove slowly home. And loved some more.

haying

Scythe to root cut, rolled backwards into time,
the hut-round ricks lashed down four-square with linen
like bonneted and faceless women.
Timothy and bromegrass so lately harvested
for yield, tripoded, teddered in sunlight, brush-hogged.
And here on frozen ground, great bales of hay
hacked free, alfalfa, oats in clover woven, pitchforked
from truck beds for the horses.
We watched them for years, their grazing.
Heartbreaking now such symmetry,
which kept our earthly house
that you or I would ever cross the windrows
of a field ripe for the haying, one or the other lost,
head high until, at last, the field raked clean
showed nothing but the seeds, crows circling,
stumps and stones, such strident fog the ghost crowds
hauling willow baskets—
cinched till their fingers bled—heads down
over the husks stalked underfoot like thorns.
I'd try on death to find you, gown made of grasses
harvest time, early, the loose hay drying in the mow,
or knit from stores of birdsfoot trifold, the greener the crop
    less packed,
heaped in the air-strung lofts of winter barns,

or scattered here in almost spring,
the last of it, what falls outside the fence clenched in my
    glove,
kicked under slats to feed the broodmares.
I have lain down across such orchard grasses on your grave
smelling the deep that keeps you, tasting snow,
something gone out of me forbidden, beyond birdsong
or vision, mantle trivial worn by the living,
there grazed wild violets, stroked fire green moss
that glows all winter clinging to the stone,
slept there on top of you, as once we'd say
a mortal lie, *I'll walk, I'll go with you.*
I've lapped your freeze and thaw,
season of wildflowers, season of leaf fall,
as close as I can get to you here on a bed of straw.

dancing with emerson

The wide pavilions of the old post road
from Western Massachusetts toward Concord
one night past three, as I drove slowly in,
just freshly plowed, were empty.
The fields flapped out on either side,
climbing the blue hills like eternity.
There at the prison rotary
I could go only round
at last to dance with Mr. Emerson.
Oh waltz with me to guardhouse radios
playing night music for the stalled,
the jailers and the jailed locked in their crimes
like songs you live by.
Mr. Emerson, hello.
Do me the honor here outside the wall
strung with barbed wire where once was meadow.
My hand in his and his about my waist
outside the gates we whirled the circle.
And so I told him, shy, with due respect,
you were my first love, Mr. Emerson.
And this was early March,
northeast the worst of months,
the snow piled high, like a rotunda.
I blizzard fated, blind and scared,

and for the first time in my life
my dance card empty.
Without a word, he such a gentleman,
who held my hand and I so lightly his
as searchlights scanned the prison yards,
and dance we did, my Mr. Emerson.
I drive that road so many seasons, drive hours
toward home or coming into Boston.
It was enough that only once we danced,
less time than it takes to slip the wire,
or dip the quill, or kiss a man.

one night in portland

I miss the old poets and their wanton ways,
outrunning, as they did, their mentors,
leaving them ravished sleeping in the temples,
to hunt, to pickax words
till crystals formed inside the wells they did dip into,
who tripped the wires, the wires every one,
bumbling, I have seen them, drunk at the podium,
lost in their poems, ravenous for applause,
banging at doors and smashing windows,
muse after muse evicted.
Bushwhacking, these who fell asleep on others' couches,
staying too long, ink on the carpets of trailer homes,
or their confused and frightened benefactors' mansions.
And once to meet together steps from the Atlantic.
For firewood they hacked up chairs and tables.
And the laughter! Like the laughter of the gods.
Oh the roaring there a meeting
of great souls, delusional, more than half mad.
Some claimed that they could cook,
soaking huge mounds of scallops in vinegar and onions,
while others of fine wine claimed to be experts
sending the bottles back at restaurants,
the steak too rare or too well done, one night in Portland.
No water from a wooden bowl for these

few of the hour assigning auras,
Pop Cat, Big Tuna, and the others,
their book read, on a shelf, or propping windows.
In smokeless rooms, the tables lit, fresh fruit, rare cheeses—
think hard on them, the ruthless death deifiers,
each a Diogenes swinging his lantern.

love letters mostly

Notes in a bottle floated up the bloodstream,
scripts hardly audible, a ringing in my ears,
love letters mostly, transfused through centuries,
once thrown from breakwaters
or cliffs. And then the writers,
unrequited, walked toward home.
Who knows how they lived out their lives,
if those they so desired did finally turn to them.
Who made me who I am.
I love to stand under an awning, smoking,
while some storm hits hard the ports of Boston.
What knows to do so dives deep as it can.

that's why he died
late spring i think to save me

Now stirred the less remembered,
too late for this,
who can no longer hold on to the worst
of it that made you whole.
Nor build a field where you can go.
It would be summer there.
At last the visitors are gone
and you alone in sunlight.
How bright a grief that found you
sitting hours till dark
and then to bed in terrible relief,
the pills left open on the dresser,
moths clinging to the curtains
as fireflies drift in.
You know it now but not as then
that death tells lies to the beloved.
Oh to be lost again, yes lost, undone,
tearing out shrubs
or digging moss, laying the stone
that racheted your hands,

no feeling finally in your fingertips.
At sunset eating out of cans,
Hair days without washing, sap-stuck,
hopelessly twisted, and heavy flown.
As when you turn a sudden to a door blown open.

dance of the seven veils

I did not pick one violet
this year nor place each small bouquet
in little china pitchers
shaped like flutes or doves.
But hid among the dandelions,
long fields of green and dandelions,
islands of gold.
Oh my sirens, my harbingers of spring.
And since I'm not Odysseus
and unafraid, my small boat sallied sideways
on the sand.
They came in droves to greet me.
I took my sisters' faces in my hands.
We crept the cliffs and sang the peasant's clock,
a rainbow locked, diphthong of lust,
peacocks' fanfare,
voices outrun the holy.
And thus we called the mighty in.
And true indeed, unfaithful every one—
the men—and who could blame them?
We were so beautiful, the very center of us edible,
our lion hair, our leaf-like swords,
all of us swinging lanterns,
dancing the dance of the Pleiades,

the seven sisters weaving silk out of our stories,
dance of the seven veils.
They thought of us—imagine—
their korasions, their robber brides.
Possessed they were and we would have it so.
And when the men, they stayed
too long, when we grew tired of them—
each fat in love, drunk on our milky wine,
we let our hair shriek white,
the filaments that shine like fog
over a dawn sea, sparks at sunrise,
ready we were to just be old again and bald.
We shook our heads, let go the seeds,
slid fast and empty to the underworld.
But as they slept across the decks,
half in, half out of hammocks, ransacked the hulls,
we did, repaired their masts.
And heaved their ships to other oceans.

another angle

Go to the other side of the table
he whispers over the body opened.
The organs, glistening, many colored shine
so like the stones of clear ponds, magnified.
Which ones to choose, wade out and keep,
place in a bowl in water at the center of a table,
which ones to skip or throw away.
Go to the other side of the table.
Imagine. We are color in the dark of ourselves
midst secrets, malignant and benign.
I watch him from a stool outside the first arena,
all of us masked. Dressed in palest green.
The body is a garden, Greek liver moss
and ivy, cornflowers; the forsythia,
smells like late summer algae.
The cells, in spite of certain death, renewing,
slick with rain. Go to the other side of the table
to find the stone unseen another angle, yellow, red,
buried, part of first fall shadow.
Look new and new and look away,
look now askance, peripherally, follow
the miles of viscera to the moon if you have to
to a long receiving line that greets you.
But go to the other side of the table.

Even the scalpel in such light is beautiful
that for a moment takes on the brilliance of the room,
my father's face, long dead, into the tissue
round the stone he is extracting,
and the scar that will heal like the meander of a river.
The organs, breathing, many colored, shine
from the other side of the table.

green

To live between the one loved and its opposite,
the body heat translating light,
spiral seed spores teeming stairs,
mantles of cells thrown off, a cape of years.
As if just breathing were an airport where
the one loved floats behind a barrier
through which, touched down, down a long corridor
you're going to pass, and no, it's not the veil
between this one life and the next.
No dream. It's not about the future.
It's simply you, you as you are, walking around the world
stealing a smoke or buying makeup,
running to catch a plane like climbing ladders
to the roof, hoisted above the one loved
and its opposite, whom you love also,
so keenly felt at times you long for a trapeze
strung through your highest trees to fly, branch-battered
and branch-bruised and sailing,
as if just breathing were the waters of the air.
Remember now that place between the dock and boat
that, sometimes, drifting out against its rope,
opened a green and holy place before the boat beat back.
But for that moment, green.
You knew me, I believe, before I knew myself.

You named me Green though you had never heard the story,
and waited for me through the long wretched death of grief,
its pale release, ongoing, whitewashed,
a statue in fountain, dry, a few green coins stuck
to the bottom—the prayers of travelers, children—
under the arch through which I'll pass
into your arms, for this white room
above the sea, almost into the other's body.

red woolen cape

Since knowing's slow when it arrives that drags its
    red woolen cape
rain-soaked and sleet-stricken, heavy on your shoulders
among a thousand trains coming or going,
hammering, like someone rattling his chains, the key of A,
as Schumann, like a deaf museum, went insane,
not in a rabble of the octaves like a child at the piano,
but in the one note A, the light of earth,
the inmates screaming a music behind glass,
the very entourage of knowing.
Say the assailant has confessed—
birds' severed heads with beaks taped shut
and each beak different from the next—
which means, the traitor knows, the bitter death of others
who in the night, as he's set free,
are shaken from their beds and hauled here.
Those who have died and who've come back
say *I knew everything I understood,*
and walk this side half ghost teeming with voices,
slipping worlds through sheets hung out to dry,
walking the corridors.
Schumann threw himself into the Rhine,
rescued *saints be praised* by ferrymen who fished him out
for two last years in the asylum,

tapping baton to podium, himself the tuning fork,

weapon or weapon-like

the A and A, the note before not the beginning,

no dreams, no possibility of passage.

His choirs, his own holy Greek chorus

whose power's to witness, not to act, whose robes are
    wine-stained, tragic,

nevertheless worn mortal night and day, the stink of hair and
    sweat and excrement.

But could they sing? It's what he begged for.

Sing to me, nature's true pupil.

now we are nine

Now we are nine, the circle of our privileged lives torn open.
True north is where our brother broke the waters
of our womb. Head first onto a marble floor,
six hours he lay alone, now we are nine.
We are nine now. Say what you like—
"What abundances of children. Nine is enough!
How spoiled you are!" Yes, spoiled.
Once we were ten in the closed circle of the bloodline.
Like you, we were as we knew life to be.
Knife in your hands, cut open destiny to feel the bloody
    waters
spill all over you. Amid the shrieking, deliver the placenta,
its blowzy gape inside which fed a life delivered.
Firstborn named Everett after his father—
what priceless rugs, rare figurines, tusks of the mastodon
    and walrus
about his death. Such are the questions of the living
who are made poor by grief. And greedy.
Stone the wife. Where was she all those hours?
Stone his son who died and robbed our brother of his will
    to live.
And so it goes, like conversations in an airport in a dream
that most forgot, flickers like sunlight through a thousand
    trees

he used to tend, spraying the apples, climbing his ladder
to pick the fruit all summer long and into autumn.
We'd board the wagon, evenings. He pulled us home,
yes pulled us, his younger brothers, sisters,
and the weight of the bushel baskets full of apples,
Henry Clay, Golden Delicious. Oh what a wedding train
of vagabonds we were who fell asleep just where we lay,
smelling all night the apple rot between our toes.
Mornings, wild-haired, we followed him out into the orchard.
Bliss of dew before Missouri heat. Dove in the moss-choked
        pond
and clutched at him. How beautiful the way he shook his hair
        from diving,
swam us ashore, smeared greenish mud against the sun
onto our faces, onto his. And so we climbed the inside
of the trees to pick the apples,
wearing, over our filth, white aprons,
apples thumping into the bushel baskets.
It might take three of us to load the buckboard, spilling
the way uphill. Too tired we were to jump the tractor,
catch the store, nor did he stop, for our sakes, that we must
        do so.

to love you

During a hurricane the waters rose, the theme park tanks, they overflowed whereby the dolphins took their chance, swam out to the sea. When all was calm again, the trainers whistled, called or sang each dolphin's name, but not a one came back. Why should they? And yet each day at four, performance time, and close enough to be seen with binoculars, the dolphins gathered for their act, circled and leapt "the fountain" straight up from the deep. As if to catch the ball they backwards dove, surfaced and lay flat nose to nose, rolled sideways in the wheel they knew so well. Little by little, though, one might just swim away and play off to the side, and then another, leaping when she should have rolled, tail skated through the hangers-on, and seemed to laugh. And so it went, day after day, the dolphins gathered. You might see two or three practicing man-taught formations. But the others had gone wild.

the house that goes dancing

Not always but sometimes when I put on some music
the house it goes dancing down through the yard
to cha-cha the willows or up into town
to tango the churches.
The neighbors, appalled, they call the police.
The dogcatcher chases my dogs up the street.
Toward the house that goes dancing in raven black boots
or enormous bed slippers,
dragging one leg like an earnest old hunchback
through the midsummer gardens gathering garlands
to wrap round her roof, she goes dancing,
love's house she goes dancing her grief-stricken dance
for his unpacked suitcases, his detritus, his hair, his hairbrush,
his glasses, his letters, his toothbrush,
his closets of clothes where I crouch like a thief
when the house it goes dancing,
a stowaway hiding in big woolen coats,
the scent of his body, the smell of him rising.
We are shaken and dragged, we are rattled
and whirled past the ending, his passing,
who waltz out of town,
all our mirrors well shattered, our china, our crystal,
our lightbulbs, our pictures have crashed from the walls.

A magnificent mess!—The doors off their hinges,
the windows wide open.
Let his spirit let go now and his big broken heart,
neither sky nor horizon, neither clay nor this dust.
It's as if he went racing his horse
past the house as we dance him goodbye
as far as we can, as we call out goodbye with our hands
round our mouths, shouting and dancing,
dancing and calling to the edge of the world
through the fields.

thank you for the poison apple

Thank you for the poison apple.
It was delicious, and the sleep,
at last, that followed.
God knows I needed it.
How many suitors waited for me there,
two, three, soon four.
Such kisses you could not imagine.
And thank you for your closets stuffed
with stolen clothes
including Demeter's black dresses,
size 5, they fit me perfectly.
As for the arsonist's light touch,
thank you. Each city that you burned
behind me lies in ashes still.
And phoenixes, not yours, will rise.
But who finds you rooting in the dust?
I am awake now in the desert.
Better we stand here face-to-face,
on the blank page
without costumes.
And if you won't come out—
know that my torment brought me
to my knees, righteous,

washed in my own hatred
and cleansed me of my bitternesses.
Goddess of retribution, I've found my calling.
Who's fairer no longer matters.
Still, look into the mirror.

south

A certain time of day, later afternoon, the sun moved over,
cooler now. I like to sit and watch the shadows of my trees
on yellow lawn. Much better than the trees themselves.
A tree will take you in, flush riot of needles light burst, the
    white pine
grown through sycamore. My heart is pounding. Leaves
exhausting. Bigger than my hand. I could lay them over
my deads' faces. And never understand why I was left alive
to brood as such far north on a back porch. How did I come
    here?
Summer's short. The sun moves like a ghost ship.
My god, they'll all come down, how many million, million.
Don't think of it. Look at the shadows brimming light
that undulate a dark, soft specificity, a southern garden
early spring, mimosa, rhododendron. It's where my birds
come from and soon will be returning, monarchs, seed spores,
western winds, my longing. I want to lie here till I'm blank
where shadows were, my hair fanned out and fallen round
    here.
Not that I want to die, only roll over, thrust my hands
into the earth and touch your shadows, summers, fathers.

a man like this

That summer he and my brothers
unload rusty barrels on the hill above the lake,
the barrels to be filled with air from a compressor
mostly on the blink to buoy up the dock
that's sagging, starboard, almost sunk.
It's a long enterprise that will take days
of sinking barrels in the shallows,
rolled out half full of water, to the hull.
My brothers dive and struggle,
drumming their heads and elbows
where the jack cranks up the far left corner,
then treading water, shaking heads
and spouting as men do in grand productions
of hard work, their little sisters watching,
drown the barrel, hoist it up between the beams.
Now the compressor's hose so many times wrapped
round with plumber's tape,
stuck in the barrel, hisses out the muck,
the remnant water, oil and stink.
My brothers wear my father's surgeon's masks
as if that helps. And so it goes,
this or some other year, except today
high on the hill one barrel tilts, set down
sideways on its own lid, perhaps,

and pitches, beating down the hill toward children
in a playpen, children in the shallows playing, mother
    shouting.
What does my father do but leap over the hill
and fly a moment, airborne over gravel trying
to catch the barrel till he falls sliding, sprawled and raked
across the stones. The babies scream.
The barrel hits the water, bobs into the cove.
Still, for a moment he is flying out beyond heroics,
willed aloft a little once above the earth.
Better such flight than consequence.
I want a man like this
who, restless, bookish, given to sudden outbursts
or affection, takes running jumps,
it would seem, all his life, against reason,
a man who flies and falls, scraped head to toe,
whose daughters wash him in the lake
with Ivory soap,
dive down to pick the rock shards
from his legs, then dry him gently off
and lay him in the Ozarks sun on a half-sunken dock
and rub his ripped and bleeding skin with ointment.

some things i say are prayers
and others poems

Some things I say are prayers and others
poems. I tell you now that I don't know
the difference, but that you—full down dead
upon a marble floor (report it now)
your sunglassed, Botoxed wife away,
your family judging, following, God forbid,
an intervention. You walked away.
I know, I know that booze or not,
I'd hold your head as you lay dying.
It is the best that we can do, keep company
with one until the end, human to human.
And all that followed was a mess,
too many Scriptures for the Darwinian,
your casket snagging on some bitter reef,
there lodged, it seemed to me, sinking
the prayers that tried to lift you up.
Nine brothers, sisters. Maybe it's best to die
alone, turn cold, cold alone, a victory.
It's not to say that I'm the only one
to understand. Perhaps I don't at all
but only claim to. Indeed I knew you little,

as much as you'd allow. You were a bastard
sometimes, kicking dogs, setting fire
to crippled teachers' shrubs, laughing,
laughing at our mother's tears.
Everett, oldest brother, you were blessed
wild. Son of the she-wolf. Romulus.
I think I never will be done with you,
never for certain who you were, what agony
or bravery or both took you, tribal genius
of the bloodline gone. Who touched you
at your birth, what teemed in you,
what faces of the ancestors, the orphans brought
aboard the miles of ice inside the cord.
The Saxon hordes stood over you, firstborn.
And first to die.

a hermit's life

Someone's made a fish pond,
small rapids dammed into a pool of stone
such stillness, save the waft of tails far at the bottom,
circles caught in sunlight, beacon to God.
The trout are yet fished out toward namelessness
in good years and in bad, drought, feast or famine,
trout free to anyone who knows the place
or comes across it in his quest for food
three quarters up the mountain.
Such was a monk's life a thousand years ago—
his gift to us—who pushed each stone flat into the clay,
spoke back to birds in their public voices,
kept silent as they gathered twigs,
threads of his own grayed tattered cloak and trousers.
And prayed God has prepared your mansions
in the purity of air. Call every creature brother,
my lambs so like a wing over my shoulder.
Oh fly into the wind that blows me back,
risking disease, contagion, a hermit's life,
combing oiled wool to make himself a blanket,
beatings and fits of loneliness born of rapt desire.
Who gives one stone is his reward.
Who gives as many stones is blessed, each one.

There are no clocks, not for five hundred years,
the air so thin you could fall off the mountain.
A saint knows not he is a saint
outside the hyacinthine hives of the deep heaven.

Call it God's will to slip upon the path,
to touch a soul and to be touched mid-air.

string game

The sea like fire, the fire like the sea,
the *like* the bridge,
the crossing over, or stepping half across

between the sea and fire.
The fire and sea. It doesn't matter.
One full of lilacs,

one full of whalers carting roses,
one full of smashed-up gleanings,
one full of peacocks,

one full of flood walls leaning,
one tidal charred planks set adrift.
A wedding dress snagged in a tree says

Take me now, or *Mayday, Mayday.*
One is a ghost ship or a shoe beside the road.
Both running back to their first home,

both pulled ahead, outgrown the wind, the faces
of the deep come before light,
the faces of the fire, eternal night

I long to know. Not death. Only a dark
to take me in.
What kills and what forgets

the terror that is hidden.
What lit up like the past, some houses in the distance.
What woman won't look back

to her two cities burning,
the rooms in which she raised her sons,
the kitchens full, the hours preparing.

Extract your hands, let go the loops
impossible to straighten.
The sea is fire, the fire is the sea.

the coat

I wore your clothes when you went out of town,
your white or light blue shirts for my pajamas.
I wear your coats now when I walk our dogs,
then we stop by to see the horses.
This coat, bought at the fair, remember,
so-called Tibetan wool, whose hood drawn tight
around my head, my hair locked up against the cold,
my heart a white flag lost among the snowdrifts.
Except today I saw a face like yours
through those last wrenched months of your long illness,
a man whose face was flying through his being,
jaundiced, hardly here, at once recognizable.
Forgive me I was happy in your coat to see you!

eating the dragon's heart

What god left for me here a dragon's heart. Resembling
    a pomegranate,
in a gold box. The parchment read *Fresh kill.*

Eat raw or braise in oil.
I lifted it from royal foil onto my best blue willow, blood
    of the ages

seeping out across the bluest bridge.
The first bite sap-like tasted of smoke-filled rooms—

women wearing smocks unloading kilns, stone sheets
    of charcoal
crushed in bowls, sprinkled with dew

drawn just that morning from high grasses. The second bite,
    sour as a lemon
eaten whole, the rind and all, the root

of Queen Anne's lace and goldenrod.
Still through the burning I began to understand what the
    crows were saying,

speaking in tongues, their news fraught with
    ill-fated warnings.
Never they choired, *be tempted to suck lifeless sweet buds*
    hung of seeds.

It is a trap. Nor smear onto this page the juice that stains
    like afterbirth
your fingers, lest you're condemned to wifery again,

lest you fall through the ice of time.
Sunk to my knees in sludge I waded bogs collecting feathers
    to be used as quills.

Then swore the pledge, kissing goodbye the last bite of my
    lover's lips.
Swallowed it whole in my green sequined dress.

Why do we offer you a dragon's heart and not a pomegranate?
To ask, one has no right to call herself a poet.

what woman

What woman talks to weeds,
who walks the gardens
like a jailer.
It's nearly fall. The few flowers,
summer-ridden, want only to die back,
go home, the earth flat as a grave,
the snows stalked windless.
Fields. Light are the dead, and careless.
There thistle, milkweed, goldenrod crushed under boot
or in my glove
smelled almost of days
the hard walks across that which would not lie down,
such bitter walks, such bitter sadness.
A widow talks to weeds
whose feet I knelt before and wept last spring,
oh anything grown green,
and picked fistfuls of dandelions,
this side the veil the great betrayers,
and spent my purse on seeds,

too early sewn, too early planted, dead
by June. And then the feast!
Armfuls of light, the season first and wildly blossoming.
What was it for?
A cemetery lot mindless of absence,
as wrenched as it's glorious.

the late rising of some small tribe

In the pine above the driveway,
birthings, droppings on the windshield
though it's September.
I must have it wrong.
It's autumn packing,
where the doves go.
You can say, on one hand,
in the end he would not eat.
I was broken, broken.
Time might put it differently.
A man has died of a fatal illness.
You held the spoon to his lips
until he turned away. Rest now.
Your work in this regard is done.

two

I'm writing two words on a husk, pure white, once covered
    in garlic cloves,
translucent fish scale penned of a sharp stick
and charcoal, pitch and rain.
I write a message that my reader, well, take *heart*.
Or shut her up, this paper like a fingernail on slate.
I'd rather hold it up before a match
to make a tiny Chinese lantern, yes. Something for me.
Some small extinction. Something for me alone.
And now it's done, passed through loose bricks.
Or say, in mortal jeopardy, I reach my hand through
bars to the girl in the cell next to us.
She has been crying night and day. And I can't sleep.
Forgive me. I've cursed her blubbering, shouted *Quiet!*
or *I'll, I'll, I'll swear you!* Not even threats
will calm her. Thank God I have a shard of mirror once sent
    to me
pressed, like a violet, in a dictionary.
Its silence says *Do what you want. Can slit your wrists.*
Can see who's coming long before the corridor rings footsteps.

Guards, sentries, wardens, guards.

It's good to have alternatives.

Death and its visions, pain or derision, a wizened foe.

Blow out the candle.

Two words I have delivered.

write a book a year

Well the wild ride into the earth was thrilling,
really, scared as I was and torn and sore.
I say what other woman could have managed it?
My life before then
picking flowers against my destiny
what glance, what meeting,
who was watching, what we don't know we know,
the hour we chose and we are chosen.
And suddenly the dead my mission,
the dark my mission.
He'd find me pounding out the hours.
Spring is for women, spring clawing at our hearts.
We are pulled forward by our hair
to be anointed in the barren garden.
I want the dark back, the bloody well of it,
my face before the fire,
or lie alone on the cold stone and find a way
to sleep awhile, wake clear and wander.

acknowledgments

Grateful acknowledgment is made to the following magazines in which many of these poems first appeared: "Love Letters Mostly" and "A Man Like This" appeared in *Brick*.

"Dance of the Seven Veils," "Don't Cut Your Hair," "Haying," and "The House That Goes Dancing" appeared in *The Kenyon Review*.

"The Birthing," "Dancing with Emerson," and "The Wind Blows Through the Doors of My Heart" appeared in *The New Yorker*.

"South" appeared in *Tufts Magazine*.

Deborah Digges was born and raised in Missouri. Her first collection, *Vesper Sparrows,* won the Delmore Schwartz Memorial Prize from New York University. *Late in the Millennium* was published in 1989, and *Rough Music,* which won the Kingsley Tufts Prize, was published in 1995. *Trapeze* appeared in 2004. Digges also wrote two memoirs, *Fugitive Spring* (1991) and *The Stardust Lounge* (2001). The recipient of grants from the John Simon Guggenheim Foundation, the National Endowment for the Arts, and the Ingram Merrill Foundation, Digges lived in Massachusetts, where she was a professor of English at Tufts University until her death in 2009.

A NOTE ON THE TYPE

The text of this book was set in Simoncini Garamond, a modern version by Francesco Simoncini of the type attributed to the famous Parisian type cutter Claude Garamond (ca. 1480–1561). Garamond was a pupil of Geoffroy Tory and is believed to have based his letters on the Venetian models, although he introduced a number of important differences, and it is to him we owe the letter that we know as old style. He gave to his letters a certain elegance and a feeling of movement that won for their creator an immediate reputation and the patronage of Francis I of France.

Composed by
North Market Street Graphics, Lancaster, Pennsylvania

Printed and bound by
Thomson-Shore, Dexter, Michigan

Designed by
Maggie Hinders

.